#RESET

Also by Amanda J. Jarratt

Overcoming Mediocrity – Fearless Women

Coming Soon

Who Am I (Children's Book)

The Lies You Tell (Romance)

#RESET

A 30 DAY TRANSFORMATION

AMANDA J JARRATT

Published by DPWN Publishing
A division of the Dynamic Professional Women's Network, Inc.
1879 N. Neltnor Blvd. #316, West Chicago, IL 60185
www.overcomingmediocrity.org
www.ourdpwn.com

Printed in the United States of America

ISBN: 978-1-7356218-0-7

About the Author

Amanda J. Jarratt was born in Petersburg, Virginia in 1984. She grew up in a small town where she loved to ride bikes, run track, and sing songs. Her imagination was bigger than anyone could have ever believed, and her spirit was filled with love, care, and passion for people. At a young age, she discovered her passion for writing. Amanda wrote her first book in the 5th grade. She entered a Young Author's contest at her school and won first place. She received a certificate and was given the opportunity to display her book in the public library.

Amanda began writing poetry and songs off and on for years until joining the Dynamic Women's Professional Network Group in 2019. Amanda was awarded the opportunity to participate in writing a collaborative self-help book. Her contribution was a chapter entitled, "Only the Strong Survive". The book was released in 2020 and quickly became a #1 Best Seller on Amazon.

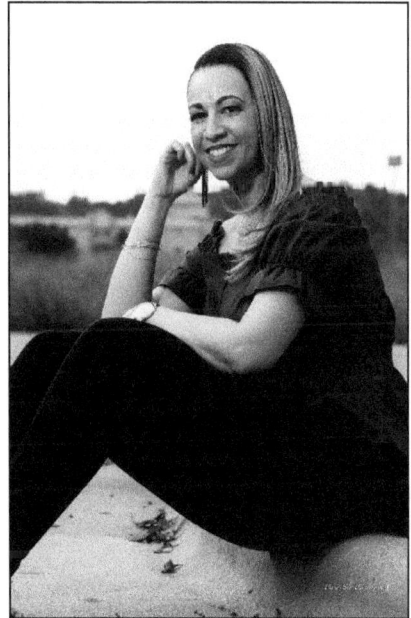

Amanda currently holds a Master's Degree in Business Administration, certifications in both Financial and HUD counseling, and a license in Real Estate. She decided there was no better time than now to focus on her passion and purpose. Amanda decided to step out on faith and release her first book to the world. She has several more to come, so stay tuned and follow her at www.hischoseninvestmentgroup.net.

Table of Contents

Introduction

What You Think Is Important

Have you ever wondered why certain people were successful? Research says, using positive words can modify your brain function by increasing cognitive reasoning and strengthening areas in our frontal lobes. In contrast, using negative words prevents certain neurochemicals from being produced which contributes to feelings of stress. Based upon this, we know there are two languages, a positive language and a negative language. According to the bible, there are several scriptures that relate to positive language.

In this quick read, I want to give you a guide on how to change your negative language into positive language. It consists of seven steps. These steps are not easy, but they are worth doing. I am not sure if you have ever heard someone say, "anything in life worth having does not come easy." Sometimes we do things out of habit or based on the influence of others. That is not always a bad thing, but what I found is that we do not always do our own research and due diligence. We just continue using the same patterns. If you get to a point where you are not getting the results that you desire, you may need to press RESET.

Pressing RESET can mean erasing or re-programming your way of thinking and your habits. It will take a lot of time, dedication, and commitment, but it is manageable. Pressing RESET can change the way you think, the way you do things, the way you speak and so much more. Once you learn how to reset your mind, everything will change. Your dreams of losing weight will no longer be a dream. Your dream of purchasing a home will no longer be a dream. Your dream of being a millionaire will no longer be a dream. Whatever your heart desires can indeed become a reality, but first we must press RESET.

Why is it important to press RESET? Well, did you know that sometimes we can block our own blessings? Yes, we can hinder ourselves from making our dreams come true. How is that? I want you to pay close attention, as I give you some examples that have occurred in my own life and how I hindered myself. Get a note pad and a pencil and prepare take some notes—you do not want to miss this!

Step 1

Controlling Your Thoughts

What are you thinking about right now? Are you thinking about work, your spouse, your kids, or bills? Are you thinking about how your plans did not work out as expected? Maybe you are thinking that it is too late for your vision or dreams to become a reality. In Proverbs 23:7, it says, "For as he thinks in his heart, so is he." So, you become what you think of yourself. For an example, if you think that you will always live paycheck to paycheck because you work a 9-5 job and no one will ever give you an opportunity, more than likely that is all you will do. Why? Well, first, you must know that no one in this entire world will give you anything. You must go and get it. If that means researching, going to school, or learning a new set of skills, then that is what it will take. You must do whatever it takes. I understand that you may be faced with many challenges; however, you must do what you have to until you can do what you want to. For an example, I was a single teenage mother of two boys. I chose to work full-time and go to college full-time because I was going to do whatever it took to make sure that I would have choices when it came to my career. I sacrificed a lot and it was truly a struggle—but I had to change the narrative.

Romans 12:2 says. "Do not conform to the pattern of this world but be ye transformed by the renewing of your mind." In other words, you must transform your way of thinking. Do not settle for someone else's opinions or thoughts of who you are or should be. Instead, think positive and think for yourself. Philippians 2:5 says, "Let this mind be in you, which was also in Christ." Therefore, let your thoughts be like Christ.

Okay. Okay, Okay. I know you want the answer to how certain people become successful, but it is important for you to understand that the first step is to control your thoughts. Honestly, do you set time out of your day to be quiet and think? You should consider setting aside 30 minutes to an hour to meditate each day. This may involve praying, thinking, reflecting, singing, and/or anything that calms you. Setting out time each day to do these things may increase positive thinking and lessen mood swings.

Have you ever known a wealthy or successful person that sleeps all day? Have you ever known a wealthy or successful person to care too much of what other's opinions are? Have you ever known a successful person not to take a risk? My point is that successful people do not do average things. They do not wake up at 8 am and they do not eat a lot of junk food. They do not watch a lot of television. They do not purchase a lot of unnecessary materialistic things. Maybe as they develop and are older, they will lean towards some of these things, but in the beginning, they realized they had to do something different than everyone else was doing in order to set themselves apart. So, what are you doing that sets you apart?

Think about this. The alarm goes off and you hit the snooze button. When the alarm goes off again, you realize you have overslept. You jump out of the bed and hurry to get dressed. You jump into your vehicle and head down the road. You probably forgot something at home, but you are already late and now you are in a terrible mood. At this point, you are feeling overwhelmed and there are a million things going through your mind. It will not take much for you to get irritated and frustrated and you may even tell someone off at work. You will probably even cut someone off in traffic too. Am I right?

For this reason, I choose to get up earlier than needed so that I can have some time to think. I need to pray and command how I want my day to go. No matter what, today will be a great day. This allows me to prepare myself for whatever may happen. I want you to try it. You must be consistent, as in anything else you do in life. Watch what happens. A simple RESET can make a huge difference.

Did you know that a thought precedes language and it is the language that communicates our thought? In other words, it is not so much of what we say that is harmful. It is what we think that is truly harmful. How so? If the thought is never there, the message would have never been conveyed. Think about it? If you never thought about something, would you speak about it? Controlling your thoughts is important just for that reason.

Matthew 4:17 says, "Changing the way you think changes your perspective which changes how you act in this world." I know exactly what you are thinking. How am I supposed to do this? This will not be as easy as it seems, right? Philippians 4:8 says, "Whatever is noble, whatever is right, whatever is pure, whatever is lovely, whatever is admirable, if anything is excellent or praiseworthy, think about such things." Do not let your mind wander to the land of negativity. Do you know what I mean? Here are some examples: "I can't lose weight," "I can't finish school," "I can't get all A's," "I can't purchase a house." Do yourself a favor. Go look in a mirror. Take a deep breath. Recite, "I can do all things through Christ who strengthens me." (Philippians 4:13). Say this until your mind has been RESET.

Suggested Prayer

Dear Heavenly Father,

I come to you on this day, asking you to help me recognize negative thoughts. Lord help me to reject all negative thinking and help me to replace it with positive thoughts. Lord fill me with happiness, peace, self-control, gentleness, patience, and understanding. Forgive me for all known and unknown sins that I have participated in. Take control of me, my body, my mind, and my soul. Today, Lord I turn all my cares over to you and ask that you would RESET me, RESET my ways, RESET my thoughts and my actions. In Jesus name I pray, AMEN.

Notes: _____

_____

_____

_____

_____

_____

_____

_____

_____

_____

_____

_____

_____

_____

_____

_____

_____

_____

_____

_____

_____

_____

_____

_____

_____

Step 2

There Is Power in Your Tongue

Now that you have learned how to control your thoughts, you must realize the power that lies in your tongue. Did you know that you can use your tongue to bring blessings and life or curses and death? The tongue can be difficult to control, but the bible tells us that with the help of the Holy Spirit, you can have power and control over your tongue. 1 Peter 3:10 says, "For whoever would love life and see good days must keep their tongue from evil and their lips from deceitful speech." It is plain and simple. If you want to experience good days, watch what you say and keep your tongue from evil and deceitful words. Colossians 4:6 says, "Let your conversation be always full of grace and seasoned with salt so that you may know how to answer everyone." See, when you converse with someone and your mind and thoughts are aligned with one another in positivity, you will be able to effectively communicate with anyone.

There is so much power in your tongue, that not only must you watch what you say to yourself, but you must watch what you say to others. Ephesians 4:29 says, "Do not let any unwholesome talk come out of your mouth, but only what is helpful for building others up according to their needs, that it may benefit those who listen." We must make sure that our words are building and encouraging others because if our words are the opposite, you will curse yourself. Do you lash out at others? Do you speak negatively to someone or about someone? If so, you are cursing yourself. It is important that you think before you respond. In some cases, you may want to take your time and formulate your conversation before-hand so that you will be certain not to curse yourself as you speak.

Have you ever told someone off? Did it make you feel good? Yes, maybe in the beginning, but later you think about it and you tell yourself, maybe I should not have said that. On another note, have you ever told someone something good? Did it make you feel good? Did it bring you joy? Did it make you smile? Did it bring the other person joy? Did it make the other person smile? Did you think about what you said and pat yourself on the back? Come on, I know that you have gone out of your way and said something nice to someone. I bet that the person had a big smile on their face. They were probably surprised. I am sure that it made their day. Think about it. When I go out to the grocery store or nail salon, I sometimes get a compliment on my hair or my nails. It usually happens when I am having a not-so-good day. It always makes me feel good that someone noticed and was kind enough to share it with me. I usually smile and politely tell them thank you, but they have no idea how much they made my day. Do you see the difference? When you speak positive things, it not only makes you look good, it makes you feel good.

You should try speaking positive things to yourself as soon as you wake up. Set your tone for the day. Tell yourself who you believe you are. Tell yourself what you believe you can achieve. Did you know that when you begin to speak positive things all day long, no matter what type of day you are having, it will still be great. For seven months straight I posted on social media, "Today is a Great Day." Each day I would add a different reason why that day was a great day. Through that process I found out how much there was for me to be grateful for. I found out that posting those positive thoughts made me feel better. It also made others feel good. It made other people realize how many things in life we neglect and forget about. I began to see a trend on social media. I saw others beginning to post a positive statement daily starting with the quote, "Today is a Great Day." I saw how easily positive messages could be spread. I chose to do that because I wanted to be able to control my day. No, I would not be able to control what happened in my day, but I would be able to control how I handled it. You should try it.

I know that this is a lot to think about, right? Listen, this is a process. You will not change overnight. The good thing about it is that you are on your way to a major change, a needed and necessary change. You now know that controlling your thoughts coincides with the power that lies in your tongue. You also know that you will need to pray and meditate on the scriptures in the bible to align your thinking with God's way of thinking. You know that the words you speak can bring life or death. So, what do you think is next?

Suggested Prayer

Dear Heavenly Father,

I come to you on this day asking you to help me realize the power that lies in my tongue. Lord, help me to remove any and every evil and deceitful word that may come to my mind. Cleanse my mind to only think of what You want me to think of and cleanse my tongue to only speak the words that You want me to say. God, help my conversations be full of grace and only speak words of life. God take control of my tongue. In Jesus name, Amen.

Notes: _____

_____

_____

_____

_____

_____

_____

_____

_____

_____

_____

_____

_____

_____

_____

_____

_____

_____

_____

_____

_____

_____

_____

_____

_____

Step 3

Speak What You Think

Now that your brain is spinning, you know you must control your thoughts and that there is power in your tongue. In this chapter, you will learn to put the two together so you can speak the words that you have controlled your mind to think.

Have you ever been told "think before you speak"? If you have, it was probably due to you saying something inappropriate. The statement implies that there was not enough thought given to see what the consequences to the words spoken might be. Can you speak without thinking? Absolutely not. The real question is, how do we plan out what words we will say?

Researchers suggest that our thoughts and speech depend on the situation. They also suggest that if the situation you are in is simple, more than likely you will plan what you will say. However, if the situation is complex, you may start with an initial plan and improvise as you go.

Okay, take a deep breath. This is a lot of information to absorb. Like, whoever thought speaking would be so hard. Proverbs 4:23 says, "Be careful how you think, your life is shaped by your thoughts." Is that not deep? Every thought that we are thinking is shaping every moment of our life. Wow! So, you mean to tell me every time I begin thinking about the things that are not working out for me, I could be shaping moments of my future? Absolutely. Therefore, it is extremely important to think and formulate what is going to come out of your mouth. How often do we speak in a hurry to respond to someone? How often do we respond without allowing the other individual to finish their sentence? How often do we really listen and take into consideration what was said?

Researchers say there is a strategy to plan what you think, but the key is to align yourself with the Word of God and how He wants you to think about things. 2 timothy 2:7 says, "Think over what I say, for the Lord will give you understanding in everything." Again, this will require stillness and time allotted to pray and study the Word of God.

Ecclesiastes 3:1 says. "There is a time to be silent and a time to speak." There are often times we say the first thing that comes to mind. We do not even really think about what we are saying. Some conversations do not require a response. Have you ever been in an argument with someone? What were you arguing about? Did the person call you names or degrade your character? Did the person challenge you in some way? What was your response? Did you call them names or degrade their character? You must know when to be silent. Trust me, I know it is so hard to do. Whenever there is negativity, whether it is a conversation or energy, you should be silent. Remember, your words can bring life or death.

I think we have gotten things twisted. How often do we feel like it is acceptable to say whatever is on our mind, regardless of whether it is hurtful or not? That is wrong. We feel like it gives us POWER, when really it shows our WEAKNESS. Self-control is the real power. Just think about it for a moment. What if you were in an argument, and instead of flying off the handle, you just stopped and listened. You stand there and look at the other person without breathing a word. How long do you think they will continue talking? Nine times out of ten they will stop. The first reason is because they will be super-shocked to see that you are not saying anything in response. It will be mind boggling to them. Secondly, they will not have anyone to argue with. Power is not about the talking aspect. True power is in the listening part. You cannot receive until you are able to listen, right? I do not know about you, but I am ready to receive whatever God has for me. Miracles, overflow, blessings, and abundance.

Do me a favor. I need you to push RESET right now. I need you to delete the myth that saying whatever is on your mind makes you powerful or strong. If you want to be powerful, learn self-control. Listen more. Speak with good intentions.

The bible assures benefits and blessings to the individuals who think before he or she speaks. Did you catch that? Let me break it down for you. You will be blessed according to your words. Wait a minute. So, all I have to do to gain God's favor and blessings is to watch my mouth? I can do that.

Proverbs 22:11 says, "He that loveth pureness of heart for the grace of his lips, the King shall be his friend." Proverbs 13:3 says, "He that keepeth his mouth keepeth his life but he that openeth wide his lips shall have destruction." Think with clarity. It is not what we speak that gets us in trouble, it is what we think.

Suggested Prayer

Dear Heavenly Father,

I come to you this day asking you to help me realize that the things in which I think will be the things in which I speak. Lord help me to remove any and every carnal thought. Remove any and every foul word that may be in my vocabulary. Help me to speak according to your word and in your will. Shape my mind lord so that my thoughts will cause me to speak in wisdom. God take control of my thinking and speaking habits. In Jesus name, Amen.

Notes: _____

_____

_____

_____

_____

_____

_____

_____

_____

_____

_____

_____

_____

_____

_____

_____

_____

_____

_____

_____

_____

_____

_____

_____

Step 4

Life or Death

Take a deep breath. Close your eyes and exhale. Are you ready to navigate through your vocabulary? You have learned the importance of controlling your thoughts. You have realized the power that lies in your tongue. You have learned that the things you think about are the things that are spoken. Now it is time to remove the vocabulary of death. Proverbs 16:13 says, "Righteous lips are the delight of kings and they love him who speaks what is right." How do we speak what is right? The answer is to get in the Word of God so that you will be in the Will of God.

Every day that you wake up, you have the chance to speak words that bring life or death. The words we choose will either tear down or build up. Proverbs 18:21 says, "The tongue has the power of life and death and those who love it will eat its fruit." This scripture is saying that everything we say, leads either to life or to death, and that which we choose we will receive. If you choose to speak in a manner that is hurtful, condemning, dishonest, or deceitful, you are choosing death. However, if you choose to speak words that are encouraging, healing, kind, and uplifting, then you are choosing life. Proverbs 12:18 says, "Reckless words pierce like a sword, but the tongue of the wise brings healing."

We live busy and hectic lives and, for that matter, it often seems negative words are easier to say. Think about it. When you are at work and someone frustrates you, what words do you say? You are driving home from a long day of work and someone cuts you off in traffic. What words come out of your mouth? Wait a minute, this is a good one. What about when your children are arguing and you are tired and have a headache. What are the words you say? I have had some not-so-good words roll off my lips when my children act up. I think the words I said put more fear into them than did the belt. Once I realized those words were cursing me, I had to switch up. I started saying things like, "Boy if you do not get out of here with that noise, Jesus come the wheel." They would look at me like I was crazy. One time I even wrote a song and played it on the piano because I was so tired of them not cleaning up. The song said, "Somebody better clean up that room before I get mad at you, somebody, somebody, somebody, SOMEBODY." Yes, I was a teenage mother, so I did things differently. They laughed about it and even sang along, but they knew they had better hurry up and clean their room.

Proverbs 4:24 says, "Put away perversity from your mouth and keep corrupt talk from your lips." Have you ever called yourself ugly, fat, stupid, or boring? Anytime you call yourself names or put yourself down, you are speaking death to yourself. Not only that, you are insulting God because He creates us in His image.

On the other hand, there are words that build up. If you choose to compliment and affirm, you are speaking life. Speaking positive affirmations to yourself is choosing life. Next time you have a disagreement with someone, instead of getting an attitude and cursing them out, just be calm, listen, and tell them God bless you. It may be hard, but I can assure you that you will feel better. You may even start laughing about it. Let me give you a few quotes that I use when I am upset. "Fix it Jesus", "Keep me near the cross", "Sweet baby Jesus", "Take the wheel

Lord". So, use these phrases to replace curse words. Watch what happens. Having control of your thoughts and words gives you power. Power is an amazing feeling.

There was a time I had to remind myself of who I was because most of my life someone belittled me. I was called all kinds of names. Whoever said that "sticks and stones may break my bones, but words will never hurt me" LIED. I began believing that I was a nobody and that I would not be able to achieve my dreams. I also began to believe I was not good enough and no one would ever love or accept me.

One day as I read the bible, God told me otherwise. I decided to put my trust in him. I started writing out who God told me I was on post-it notes. I hung those notes all around my mirrors, tv, and bedframe. People that visited me laughed and thought it was crazy. Some people even said I should take them down. I kept it up until they got so old they began to fall off. It did not matter who I came in contact with or where I was at, I knew who I was. When I came in contact with people that treated me less than I deserved, I would begin speaking out the affirmations that I wrote down. That would remind me of my worth and how I was supposed to be treated. I began refusing to speak or receive negative words into my space because it reflects death. It might not cause a physical death, but it will surely kill your mental space. For example, we have all heard someone say, "Come on, you are killing my vibe." Sometimes we must take the time to hit the RESET button. Speak positive things because it will bring life into the atmosphere. I want you think about who you are and write it out. Speak those things over your life every day. Choose life.

Ephesians 5:19-20 says, "Speak to one another with psalms, hymns, and spiritual songs. Sing and make music in your heart to the Lord, always giving thanks to God for everything." Let us think before we speak so that our words can build one another, encourage, and inspire one another. No matter what happens, give God the praise. In His word He tells us that.

Suggested Prayer

Dear Heavenly Father,

I come to you on this day, asking that you will remove all words of evil and death from my vocabulary. Give me words full of life. Allow me to speak to others including myself that will build and encourage. God take control of my lips, that each word spoken would be uplifting. In Jesus name, Amen.

Notes: _____

_____

_____

_____

_____

_____

_____

_____

_____

_____

_____

_____

_____

_____

_____

_____

_____

_____

_____

_____

_____

_____

_____

Step 5

Speak It Into Existence

Do you believe in what you say? Think about it. Have you ever said, "I am going to be a millionaire?" When you speak, are you saying it aloud or do you really believe it deep down in your heart? Do you speak with hopefulness? Think back to the last time you spoke about something you wanted to happen. Did you playfully speak about it, or did you speak about it in determination?

Quick example. Years ago, I was in the restaurant industry and I started as a shift manager. I knew I possessed the qualities and skill set to be the operations manager, and I desired the role. I told myself that one day my picture would be on the wall and my name would be on the business cards as the leader of that establishment. I took the role seriously and I knew in order to get the corporate leaders to pay attention I had to be different. Different like bold different. I began coming to work and operating it as if it were mine. I gave lots of suggestions to reach out business goals and built the morale with the team. Although, I was not getting credit for the results, I continued to pursue my dream. I came in every day with a smile on my face and I pushed the team to reach its goals. I would often run contests for meeting expectations with the reward of lunch that I bought out of my own pocket. My direct supervisor began to see the changes and received recognition from the top leaders. He decided to give me a raise. In fact, I ended up getting three raises in one year. I moved to the next position, which was the assistant manager, but that was not where I wanted to end my journey. I had a cut-and-clear plan. When the corporate leader would send emails, I would reply and sign with "Future Operator." They picked up on that quickly and they themselves began to believe that I could be the next leader in line. One day I got an email from the CEO and, to my surprise it read, "Dear Future Operator." I smiled and, in that moment, knew my efforts had been successful. See, I had sent them signed messages so much that they took it upon themselves to do the same thing. I knew my hard work and dedication was paying off. It also helped that I was speaking things into existence. I even took it up a notch when I began to write and sign a title that I did not even possess yet. It may seem or sound crazy, but I had to be BOLD and I had to RESET my mind and way of thinking. Nonetheless, I became the Store Operator. See, there is a difference between saying something and believing something. Have you ever spoke over your life like that before?

Here is another example. I was in a time of need financially. I was making an offer on a property for my client and received the news that I had lost the bid. I was heartbroken. I was devastated. I was depending on that commission check. I cried. But then I remembered how my words could play a part in the result. I took out my check book and business card. I placed them on the table, and I began praying over them. I asked God to cause a minor incident that would allow me to win the bid. That was a bold prayer being that the bid was already over. Three days later, I received an email saying that the buyer backed out and I was now in control of the bid. I had already told my client we lost. Imagine me calling him back to tell him, oops my bad, we won. He asked how in the world that happened. I replied, prayer. He had no idea that PRAYER was the real reason. I believed that if I spoke over my situation God would shift things. He did.

Are you with me? It is extremely important that you speak about your desires with passion and belief. Of course, this will take a lot of practice and discipline. Isaiah 55:11 says, "So shall my word be that goes out from my mouth, it shall not return empty but it shall accomplish that which I purpose, and shall succeed in the thing for which I sent it." In other words, whatever I speak must manifest because I will not allow it to come back void. The bible tells us we must believe in our heart what we ask for and have faith that it will happen.

Whether you know it or not, we have all spoke something into existence. Okay, remember when you were riding down the highway and saw the mega million billboard and said, "Oh, one day I will hit the lottery?" Do you remember now? Now you may not have seen it manifest, but you did speak it. Maybe not a great example, but my point is, if you put forth the actions in which you want something to take place, it could really happen. I have said things like, "I am going to buy a house" or "I am going to get that bonus on my job." Guess what? I did both. However, I did not just speak it into the atmosphere and let it sit. I spoke daily and I began to do whatever was necessary to make it happen. I think we sometimes get confused. We think that all we must do is say it. Not true. The bible tells us that faith without works is dead. Speaking things into existence plays a major role in the psychological aspect. Remember, it starts with our thinking, right? Once we can reset our mind and align it with our words, things begin to manifest. I want you think about one thing you want to accomplish. Write it down. Say it every day aloud. Do your due diligence. Write beside the goal a list of things you must do to reach it.

Psalms 33:9 says, "For he spoke and it came to be, he commanded and it stood firm." God is instructing us on how to speak daily but we must take heed and believe. We must speak about the things we want so much that they happen. If you focus your attention on something long enough, it will have to manifest in some form or another.

Suggested Prayer

Dear Heavenly Father,

I come to you on this day asking that you will allow everything I speak to come into existence. Lord change my thinking and speaking habits that I may speak things which are pleasing to your ear. Help me to understand how important my vocabulary is. Lord fix my heart that it may be pure. God fix my mind so I may believe in what I am speaking. God take control of my mind and mouth. In Jesus name, Amen.

Notes: _____

_____

_____

_____

_____

_____

_____

_____

_____

_____

_____

_____

_____

_____

_____

_____

_____

_____

_____

_____

_____

_____

_____

_____

#RESET

Step 6

Watch It Manifest

We have learned how our thoughts lead our brains in speaking either negative or positive words. We have also learned how powerful our tongue is and how we speak the things we think about. We also learned that our words are categorized in life-or-death terms. Lastly, we learned how to speak things into existence so we can now watch it manifest.

Now, how many of you know there is no such thing as an expiration date when it comes to watching things manifest?

See, sometimes we ask God for something or declare and decree something to happen, but if it does not happen as fast as we want it to, we give up. Let me tell you a secret. Everything is a process and will take time.

The bible tells us that if we ask and believe in something, we will receive it. It also says to be clear and specific on what you want. You must believe that things will manifest by acting as if you already have it.

Psalms 37:4-5 says, "Trust in the lord with all of your heart and He will give you the desires of your heart." "Commit everything to the Lord, trust in Him and He will watch over you." The bible tells us that the key is to trust in God and allow Him to work out all the details. So, if you want to watch things manifest, you must first check yourself.

There is no greater feeling than watching things you have prayed for, sacrificed for, and believed for, manifest. I remember the day I bought my house. I felt like a billionaire driving into my garage for the first time. Clicking the garage opener felt magical. Walking in the house with high ceilings and fresh new carpet, I was in awe for months. I would literally lay in bed at night for hours looking up at the ceiling and thanking God. Six months later I went to a dealership and bought a new car for the very first time in my life. I felt like I was driving a Bentley. Smiling ear to ear with the radio blasting and my sunroof open, I was in heaven. It was a process and it did not happen overnight. If I can be honest, it started with me controlling my thoughts because people said I would NEVER be able to do it alone. They were right. God came through big time. I had to realize how much power my tongue holds. Instead of me believing people and believing the circumstances that I was in, I decided to trust God. I can do all things through Christ who strengthens me.

Do not get me wrong. Things did not magically appear. It took time. It took hard work. It took me constantly telling myself that I could, instead of saying I could not. Despite the many obstacles I faced, I still spoke life. Manifestation comes once the process has been completed. Therefore, do not rush. Do not miss a step. Missing a step could cause delays in you receiving the manifestation.

Let's do a quick check list. Are your thoughts controlled? Have you changed your mindset? Do you know how much power is in your tongue? Are you speaking before you think? Do you speak words of life or death? Do you believe in what you say? Do you trust God? Are you specific and clear in what you ask God for? Are you in a position to receive? Do you have the right intentions and motives? Once you can successfully check these things off, get ready to watch the manifestation of God.

Suggested Prayer

Dear Heavenly Father,

I come to you on this day asking you to guide my every thought. I ask that you take control of every word I choose to say so I may watch the manifestation of your works. Give me strength and courage to endure the process. God, take control of the situation and teach me to lean on You and not mine own understanding. In Jesus name, Amen.

Notes: _____

_____

_____

_____

_____

_____

_____

_____

_____

_____

_____

_____

_____

_____

Step 7

Changing Your Language Will Change Your Life

Do you want your life to change? We have learned the process of changing our thoughts and vocabulary, but in order to change your life, you must be consistent. Anyone can speak or think positive once, but can you do it enough that your entire life changes?

Researchers say that every thought we have is a vibration, and the key to maintaining positivity is to learn how to change our state of mind. Researchers also say there are several ways to change your state of mind. They say that when you feel like you are on top of the world, you send out a matching frequency and you attract positive people. Think about it. When you get a new job, new home, new car, or a new significant other, you display a certain glow, a positive energy that attracts like-minded individuals. People will be drawn to you and inspired by you.

The last time you lost a job, gained weight, or broke up with your mate, you displayed a different type of energy. This energy was negative and unattractive. People probably chose not to be around you and wondered what happened to the happy-go-lucky you. So, how do we change our language permanently? It starts here.

In Matthew, chapter 12, verses 34 and 35, Jesus reminds us that the words we are speaking are actually the overflow of our hearts. When one becomes a Christian, there is an expectancy that a change of speech follows because living in Christ makes a difference in a person's choice of words. The bible tells us that becoming a Christian will require a change. We must remove old habits and develop new ones. The bible gives us 12 specific steps to show us how to change and improve ourselves to become what God wants. You must change your purpose in life by loving and dedicating yourself to God. You must believe you can change with God's help by trusting Him. Study the bible. Repent of your sins, as repentance is a change of mind. Develop a plan of action by creating a check list of steps you will take to change. Pray regularly, as you should pray for forgiveness and pray for God's help. Seek help from other Christians, as they can offer encouragement. Practice what is right until it becomes second nature. Change your bad habits to good habits. Avoid temptation by changing the habit. Changing the habit will sometimes require changing your friends. You must face one day at a time. Last and not least, be patient, as it is a process.

God provides every tool we need to change. It is up to us to determine to follow his will. Are you ready to press RESET? Once you have reset the way you think and speak, I can assure you that your life will change for the better. I believe in you. I know for a fact, if you follow these steps, endure the process, and stay the entire process, you will be a changed creature in Christ. So, say it with me, "RESET."

Suggested Prayer

Dear Heavenly Father,

I come to you on this day asking that you help me to be consistent in the process of changing my life. Help me to understand that this is a process, and it is in your time that I will see the manifestation of your work. Help me to change all my ways, that they will be pleasing to You. God take control of my life that it will never be the same. In Jesus name, Amen.

Notes: _____

_____

_____

_____

_____

_____

_____

_____

_____

_____

_____

_____

_____

_____

30 Day Transformation

Have you ever heard of fasting? Most people have done a fast, whether it was for religious reasons or weight loss. There are several types of fasting techniques. Some people fast from social media, junk food, meat and so on. They choose a time frame in which they will refrain from these activities. The purpose behind it is to gain something. It could be insight. It could be weight loss. It could even be for God to answer a prayer. So, what I want you to do, is take 30 days to fast. Research says it takes 21 days to break a habit. We want to make sure we break these bad habits, so we are going to take 30 days. In those 30 days, I want you to switch it up. If you normally wake up right on time, I want you to start setting your alarm for an hour earlier than usual. I want you to lay there for the first 15 minutes. I want you to thank God for waking you up. I want you tell God what kind of day you want to have. I want you to recite or call out each affirmation that fits your life. I want you to put on an inspirational song. Close your eyes and sing along. Get up and look in the mirror. Recite those affirmations again. Play another inspirational song. Now go get ready for your day. The work has already been done. You have already commanded your day. Your day will be greater than great. Why? Because you spoke it into the atmosphere. You commanded what was going to happen. You already shifted your spirit. Now, although something may happen that you do not expect, no weapon formed against you will prosper. You may be caught by surprise, but your spirit is ready. You are ready.

We are off to a good start. We have shifted our focus and our mind. As you get into your vehicle, I want you to do one of two things. Either put on some inspirational music for the duration of the ride to work or ride in silence. If you choose to cut on the inspirational music, I want you to sing along. Cut it up loud. It does not matter if you cannot sing. No one can hear you but God. Sing it like you wrote it. Sing it like you are at a concert with a million people. Sing it like your life depends on it. Let it saturate your vehicle, mind, and soul. If you choose to ride in silence, I want you to use that time to reflect out loud who you are and where you want to go in life. Recite your affirmations. Play your favorite hype jam just as you turn into the workplace. My favorite hype jams are "You Must Not Know 'Bout Me" and "To the Left, To the left," by Beyonce'. Although she is referring to a break-up, you can use the words in about any conversation or topic. Sometimes I have to remind myself of who I am. Sometimes I have to remind others as well. Alright, so now we are ready to cook with grease. Go into work with a huge smile on your face. Walk in like you own the place. Be so confident that others want to know what kind of coffee you drank. Continue your day being bold, confident, and hyped because you know who you are. You know what you bring to the table. This applies to all fields. It does not matter if you clean houses, sell cars, or run the drive-thru at Hardees. Be the best cleaner, salesman, cashier that there is. Hum in your mind your favorite hype jam. If something happens that throws you off track, stay calm. Take deep breaths. Use your non-cursing quotes that I provided you to let off steam. If you have to, go to the bathroom. Look in the mirror and remind yourself of who you are. Recite your affirmations. Tell yourself today is still greater than great.

Alright. We made it through the workday. It is time to go home. I want you to do the same thing that you did this morning on your way to work.

Play an inspirational song and sing along the duration of your ride home or ride in silence while reflecting. If you choose to reflect, call out all the things that you felt went wrong. For each thing that you did not like, I want you to look at it with the "glass half full instead of half empty" point of view. That means, think about the bad part and find something good in it. I know that may seem weird so let me give you an example. I visited the nail salon not too long ago. The owner was telling me how bad her day was going. I asked why and she stated that one of her shelves that was full of product fell off the wall. She said her products went flying everywhere. I asked her if anyone got hurt. She replied no. I asked her if any of the products were damaged. She replied no. It was not that bad of a day then, I replied. The shelf fell and made a mess, but no one got hurt and the products were not at all damaged. If it had been a completely bad day, the shelf would have fallen on someone causing an injury or lawsuit. The products could have been damaged and caused her to lose inventory and have to re-purchase new product. We must learn to see the good in the bad. For God says that He is working out everything for our good.

Okay. We made it home. Head to the bathroom and take off those clothes. Run the shower or the bath. As you get in, start to close your eyes, pray and thank God for safe travel and allowing you another opportunity to get right what you got wrong yesterday. Thank him for allowing today to be greater than great. After dinner, homework, or whatever routine you have, take 30 minutes to an hour before bed to write down what was different today verse yesterday. If you have not started working on your list of goals or creating your vision board, work on them. Each night you should take some time to work on YOU. Revisit your dreams, goals, and visions. Before you go to bed, recite your affirmations. Pray that tomorrow will be easier than today and if it is not, pray that God give you the strength to endure it.

You now have 30-day formula, a "fast" that needs to be implemented consistently. This is not a gimmick. This will not change anything if you are not willing to do it for a complete and consecutive 30-day period. You cannot skip a day or a week. When you skip days or weeks, you allow the old habits to creep back in and take over. That means you will have to start all over from scratch. It is just like a diet or exercise plan. You cannot do a Keto diet for a week and skip a week and expect to get the same results someone that does a keto diet consistently. You should spend more time on YOU than you do on social media following people or watching television. Your primary focus should be fixing YOU. Resetting your mindset and changing your habits should be the primary focus. How can you fix YOU if your focus is on everything and everyone else? You *must* focus. You *must* re-program your way of thinking. If you can follow these steps that I have given to you for 30 days STRAIGHT, I can assure you that you will be in a much better place mentally. You will begin to think differently. You will be more confident. Your perspective will change. Things that were so important will no longer be of importance. Why? Because your mind has shifted. You have realized the things that are truly important. You will want to spend more time becoming a better you because the old ways were holding you back from your true potential. Guess what will matter? Your PEACE. Your SAFETY. Your HEALTH. Your FINANCES. Your DREAMS. Watch and see. You must be CONSISTENT. 30 days of new habits. Out with the old and in with the new. Are you ready to break bad habits? Are you ready to RESET your mind? Are you ready to be your best you?

Notes: _____

_____

_____

_____

_____

_____

_____

_____

_____

_____

_____

_____

_____

_____

_____

_____

_____

_____

_____

_____

_____

_____

_____

_____

_____

_____

#RESET

Day 1	Day 2	Day 3
Day 7	Day 8	Day 9
Day 13	Day 14	Day 15
Day 19	Day 20	Day 21
Day 25	Day 26	Day 27

Day 4	**Day 5**	**Day 6**
Day 10	**Day 11**	**Day 12**
Day 16	**Day 17**	**Day 18**
Day 22	**Day 23**	**Day 24**
Day 28	**Day 29**	**Day 30**

#RESET

Daily Affirmations

1. I am who God says I am.

2. I am more than a conqueror.

3. I am strong.

4. I am fierce.

5. I am bold.

6. I am loved.

7. I am anointed.

8. I am His chosen.

9. I am the lender and not the borrower.

10. I can do all things through Christ who strengthens me.

11. I am the head and not the tail.

12. I will live and not die.

13. I will WIN.

14. I am blessed.

15. I am favored.

16. I am protected.

17. I am anxious for nothing.

18. I am ENOUGH.

19. I am beautiful.

20. I am smart.

21. I am a millionaire.

22. I am healed.

Now you try it. Write a list of things that you know yourself to be.

1. _____

2. _____

3. _____

4. _____

5. _____

6. _____

7. _____

8. _____

9. _____

10. _____

Goals:

Take some time to write your goals down and what you will do to accomplish them.

_____

_____

_____

_____

_____

_____

_____

_____

_____

_____

_____

_____

_____

_____

_____

_____

_____

_____

#RESET

Actions:

What actions should you partake in to reach your goals? Write them here.

_____

_____

_____

_____

_____

_____

_____

_____

_____

_____

_____

_____

_____

_____

_____

_____

_____

_____

_____

Habits:

What habits are preventing you from being the best you can be? Write them here.

_____

_____

_____

_____

_____

_____

_____

_____

_____

_____

_____

_____

_____

_____

_____

_____

_____

_____

#RESET

Prayers/Scriptures:

Keep track of your prayer time. What are your favorite scriptures? Write them here.

_____

_____

_____

_____

_____

_____

_____

_____

_____

_____

_____

_____

_____

_____

_____

_____

_____

_____

_____

Vision Board

Sometimes it is more helpful to see pictures. Create a vision board. Grab some old magazines, scissors, and glue. Place pictures and words that describe what you want to be, where you want to go, and/or what you would like to have. Once you have completed it. Hang it up. Look at it every day. Make sure that you are checking the actions off on your check list as you complete them. Stay encouraged. This is a process, remember. You may want to create a separate vision board entitled, "Reset." On this vision board, place pictures or words that describe how you can change your habits and reset your thinking. Hang them up. Grab some post-it notes. Write down your affirmations and hang them up all around places you constantly visit. You will not be disappointed. Okay, you are on your way to a happier and healthier YOU. All you must do is press RESET.

Notes: _____

_____

_____

_____

_____

_____

_____

_____

_____

_____

_____

_____

_____

_____

_____

_____

_____

_____

_____

_____

_____

_____

_____

www.ingramcontent.com/pod-product-compliance
Lightning Source LLC
LaVergne TN
LVHW051800080426
835511LV00018B/3367